"Where Whispers Echo"

by

Nasreen Latif

AF658151

BlueRose ONE.com
Stories Matter

First Published in July 2022

ISBN: 978-93-5704-214-7

BLUEROSE PUBLISHERS

www.bluerosepublishers.com

info@bluerosepublishers.com

+91 8882 898 898

Typographic Design:

Sachvesh

Distributed by: BlueRose, Amazon, Flipkart

Born 13th February, 1960....Am a Mother of a beautiful young and successful Lady. My passion is reading and writing any worthwhile material that suits me. I studied Literature in high School, One of my favourite subjects. I was conversant in English though the Language wasn't my Mother Tongue.

I was a member of many poetry groups on G+, (a Google App) where I mastered the Art of writing Poems in various forms. I would enjoy the various Poems until one day I decided to Pen my on thoughts in Poetry.

Poems give me a sense of ME, my feelings, My thoughts, My Pain and Tears from a disturbed past...A broken Heart... My sense of identity...A lose of a parent (Dad), I felt my life had come to a stop, and a hopeless relationship that was always on the Rocks...

Poems written in this Anthology are mostly Freestyle, Haikus, Couplets and Free verse. Every new Poem creates a deep excitement in my Mind, anxiously awaiting for me to Pen it down before it vanishes from my thoughts.

My entire Life is my child who is the light of my Eyes, to whom I dedicate this Anthology of Poems. My happiest moment was when my daughter was born on 13th February, 1993. We share a birthday. I have kept her close to my Heart ever since...The joy and smile on my face!

Am fascinated by Life on the whole....My conscious compels me to write on Passion, joy, grief and any emotions that may carry a message in my Mind. Every inspiration has a reason, A Child's Tears....The Pain behind the Sorrow... Maybe Hunger or despair, a broken Heart, a Street Child, a Mother, a Baby in the Womb...

Am fascinated by the Weather...The Snow in Winter when all Trees and Plants die. Spring brings in endless vibrant colours, Trees, Shrubs and Plants bursting into greenery and blossoms. Summer brings Sunshine, joy and happiness. Just when am beginning to enjoy the hot Weather, Autumn jumps in bringing a cold spell and most Leaves turning Hues of Bronze, Yellow and Gold.

My name depicts a Wild Rose (Nasreen - A Persian name). My favourite blossom is a Rose, especially Red Roses. 'Every Rose is an essence of Love'. My Poems on Roses depict happiness, love, tears and a broken Heart. Daisies and the Sacred Lotus are my favourite Flowers too. Am fascinated by the Lotus Flower as it changes colour through out the Day, from Purple to Blue, Pink to Yellow.

Travelling is a Hobby and I tremendously enjoy the Wildlife and the African Savannah. Africa is Vast and My country Kenya has it's on collection of much adored Wildlife and Birds. Am fascinated by the Pink colour of the Flamingos, lining the various Lake shores. Lake Nakuru National Park is my favourite Park, being in my hometown. Luckily, I often get to see the Migration of millions of Flamingos.

Writing Horror Poems is my Passion...I enjoy a bit of Thrill and 'that Fear' that engulfs me and the Goosebumps as my imagination runs deep and Wild...

I look at Life on the perspective of 'Life and Death'...Life is too short to accomplish our dreams. 'Time wasted is time lost forever'.

A Girl child is a foundation for a future generation.. When a Girl child is born, in some communities there is happiness and in some there is sadness, for some it's an abomination and thus a 'Girl Child' is terminated in the Womb. 'The innocent female Seed'.... What wrong did she ever do to deserve death in the Cradle!?

My dedication goes to **Saher Malik,**

♡♡♡♡♡♡

The blossom from my Garden
The fragrance to my Soul
The joy of my Heart
The Jewel of my Crown
The Light in my Eyes
The love of my Life
My reflection in all sense
'If I ever found happiness than it was You'

♡♧♡♧♡♧♡♧♡♧

Table of Contents

The old Baobabs

Dreaming of a deep Jungle
Getting restless as I pass Giant Baobabs

A mysterious atmosphere surrounding me
Tossing and turning in deep sleep

A lone figure
Wait! That looks like me!?

My confused Mind
The Giant Trees appear scary

With branches like Roots
As if trying to grab me

Fear gripping me
My Heart in my Throat

A Foggy Evening
The Sun has set a while ago

Whichever direction I take
Giant BAOBABS line my Path

~nasreen

A Flicker of Light

As evening persists
A flicker of Light giving me company

The Lantern sitting on a Shelf
Light dancing to the Wind

Sitting alone in my Cabin
Lighting a Fire in the Chimney

A cold chill bellowing against the Wooden Walls
A Wolf in the distance howling away

Frightening thoughts cross my Mind
What if the creature breaks in ..!?

I would be left with a Story to be told
Or no Soul would ever know

~nasreen

Wild Daisies

Little White Heads bobbing up
Like beautiful Buttons, Yellow and White
Am tempted to pin a few in my Locks

~nasreen

KNOWLEDGE

Knowledge

In the Ocean of Knowledge
I followed my quest into the unforeseen
'Well Here I am ..!'

~nasreen

Dawn

That beautiful moment at Dawn
The first Rays of Sunshine
Bursting into Yellow and Orange Hues

~nasreen

Loneliness

Green Pastures and a Single
Daisy
Standing tall amongst the Grass
Reminding me of my loneliness

~nasreen

Creepy Shadows

A Jungle of Bare Trees
Looming Shadows that frighten
Ohhh....Fearfully horrific!

~ nasreen

CHANEL

Red Lipstick

That deep Red colour
The Red Lips, the colour of my Lipstick
Seducing his Ego

~ nasreen

Moonlight

Beautiful is the Wonder in the Sky
It's glow more powerful than a Street Lamp or a Torch

Even a blazing Fire is no comparison
Not even Flashlights

There is Magic in the Night Sky
The Moonlight makes me want to Whisper

To sing a Heart touching Melody
The soothing calmness

The cool Breeze over the Ocean
The glow of the Moonlight sparkling over the Water

Mesmerising nightfall
How many fathoms deep is the Sea ?

Not a single Giant Wave rolling
The Tide so calm

Little Crabs running on Sandy Beaches
Tiny Sea creatures drifting ashore

Ohhh Beautiful Moon
You make me forget my loneliness... You bring Peace!
And tranquillity

~nasreen

African Sunset

Beautiful African Sunset
Different hues of Yellow and Orange filling the Blue Sky

The Sun seems to be going down fast over the Horizon
Dusk looming

Creepy Crawlies singing their Song
A thousand sounds filling the evening Skies

Crickets and Grasshoppers
A Spider or Two crawling over the Savannah

A lone Lion watching the Woodlands
Probably expecting a Prey to pass by

An awful silence filling the Air
Final White Clouds disappearing in the Evening Sky

Stars appearing
Suddenly I see a shooting Star

A wishful night it seems
What I need is a Bonfire to keep the animals away

A Laughing Hyena's cackle filling the Air
Ohhh that silly Beast Always chasing after Dead Prey

Shadows of the Acacia Trees surrounding me
Am in time to see the Lion's hunt, The ignorant Beast
of Prey

~nasreen

Stop Stop

A journey into the unknown
Someone shouts STOP...! STOP...!
Fear grips me as I see Giant Hands in the Fog

~ nasreen

The Three Weary Travellers

Morning Rise in the Sahara Desert
A cool breeze touching the Souls of the three herds
Men

Laying prostrate on the Sand to the Almighty
Only a prayer Mat under their tired Feet

Such peace and tranquillity embrace them
How beautiful a moment it was to my Eyes?

Camels silently grunting away chewing Cud
Laying down in Prostration too

~nasreen

Romance

Love' You found me over the Bridge
A sweet Rhapsody of the Hearts
I' Melting into the Arms of my 'Lover...'

~ nasreen

A Cold Day

A Windy Cold day it was
Standing alone on the Seashore

Watching Boats gliding on the surface
People swimming in a Sea of calmness

My disturbing thoughts
Ohhh Yess...Just my disturbing thoughts!

Seems like I was the only one with a disturbed Mind
Looking over the Horizon

Dusk setting in and a cold chill
How I wished for his warmth around me

I seemed to have stood alone like forever
Dreaming an unfulfilled dream

Life's turning points
Always getting the better of me

Love bounds one to untold Emotions
Tearing at the Heart and Soul

~nasreen

Ghost Ship

Sailing along the Pacific Coast
A Foggy Dawn bringing a surprise
A Ghost Ship spotted by Seafarers

~ nasreen

Sheer Beauty

Beautiful Lotus bobbing on a Pond
Am mesmerised by it's colours

Pink for Sunrise
Yellow for Mid-day

Lilac for evening
Blue for night

This sacred beauty from the East
Having mysterious Powers

A perfect analogy to Life
Growing in Murky Waters

Am tempted to pluck one
Pinning in my Hair

~nasreen

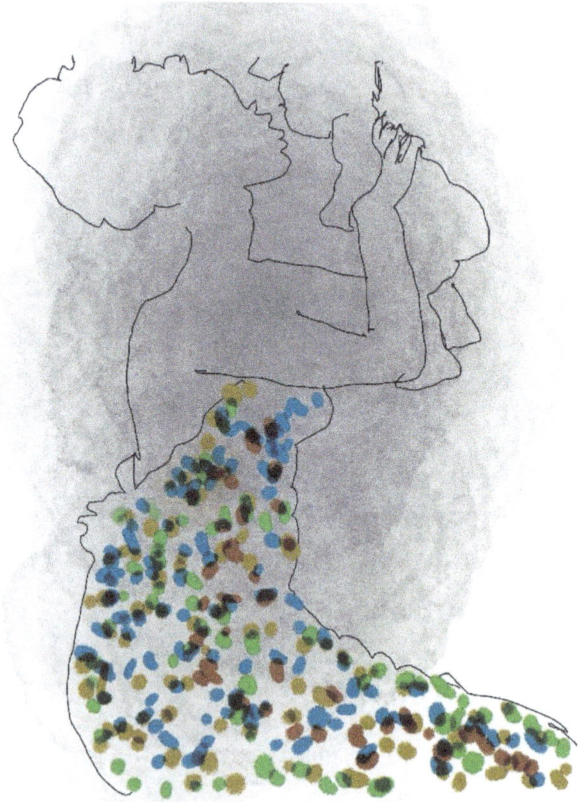

The Womb

Nine months in another Body
A Life sustaining Womb

A miraculous birth into this Life
Giggle and cheer I hear around me

My Mama's laughter
Her joyful singing and humming

Loving hugs and Kisses
Cuddles to make me sleep

My sweet Angel
My mom

~nasreen

The Phantom Train

Speeding away from Waterloo Station
On a cold chilly night a Phantom Train, the year 1947
Just Lights in a Single Cabin but No occupants
Am I having a Nightmare !?
I pinch myself

~ nasreen

RAPE

The horrific Word "RAPE"
Tearing a Woman from the Soul
The pain that can never heal

~nasreen

Dancing the night away

Dancing the night away
His Hands reaching out

Beyond my Belly Button
His sweet caress awakening my sensuality

Music that thrilled my senses
Soft Kisses occasionally

Sweet murmurs into my Ears
Nibbling at the softness

Mmmmmmmmm...My sweet Lover
Arms around the Waist

Dancing to the Love symphonies
Every heartbeat asking for more

His peering Eyes
As if questioning 'Do you love me .!?

Only my Soul answering to his intimidating Eyes
Making me blush at his piercing looks

Ohhh beautiful Soul
Sing me our Love song

Say 'You love me...'
Let me hear the whisper 'I love you...' I love you...'

~nasreen

Shadows of the past

Like my past as I walk under the Canopy of the Trees
The Wind Whispers a Melody

Ringing a Bell in my Mind
One time old favourite

How would the Trees know !?
Why would they Whisper !?

As a Child I would play besides the River
Ohhh how I loved the Park .

Nature in full harmony
Creatures of the Park busy in their hideouts

Such serene beauty
Now just a Shadow of my Past

How time flies
Sadness fills my Heart

Many are no longer
The old Souls my Friends

As I walk under the old Trees
A breeze whispers

Come with me... Come with me gentle Soul ...
Let's walk together what's left of us

~nasreen

Nature

Such awesome beauty
Only Nature Prevails on Mother Earth
Tears of joy cries the Soil when it blossoms

~nasreen

Colours Colours

Splendid scenario in a Street
A Rainbow has descended upon me
Amazing splash of different Hues of Coloured
Umbrellas

~ nasreen

A Windy Day

Summer's Sun burning overhead
A Windy Day in the Garden
Blossoms flying all over

~nasreen

Another Sunset

Lost Camels in the Desert
In search of an Oasis
To quench their thirst

~nasreen

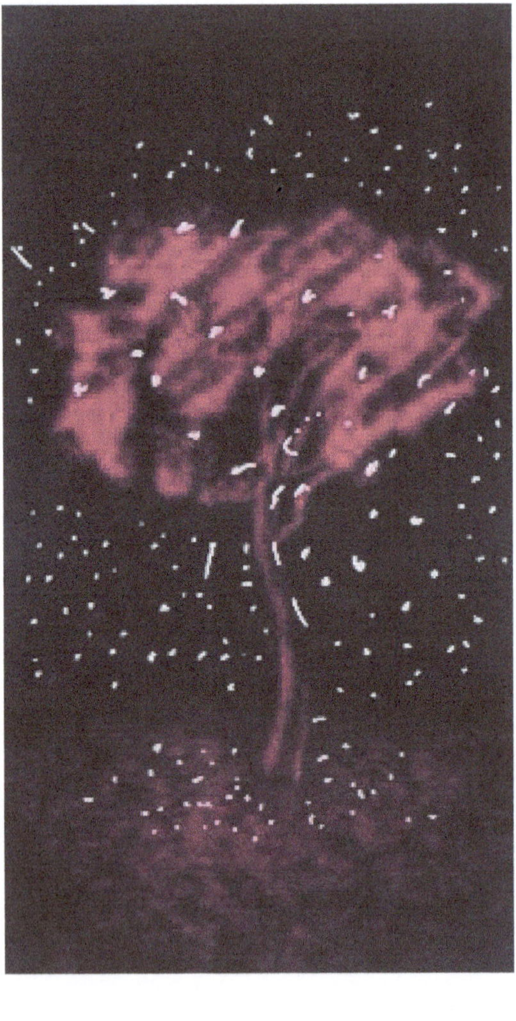

Stardust

Gazing upon the Sky
A beautiful Magical Starlit night
Sprinkling Dust of happiness everywhere

~nasreen

The Single Rose

Dreams Dreams Dreams
Beautiful imagination or an illusion
The Prince in shining Armour
Did he just sweep me off the Floor !?
Love confusing my thoughts
Long waits at the Harbour
His Ship never docked
Sleepless nights
Lonely nights
Seeking warmth in the wrong Arms
Love's betrayal or lust

~nasreen

My Garden

Trees and Birds
Creepy crawlies and a Fish Pond

Red Beauties falling from Trees
Ohhh ..Making my Heart sing

Under the Canopy of the Tree
Apples and more Apples

Reminding me of Blushing Faces
And Pink Cheeks

Nature's unexplainable Beauties
'Am taking a bite of an Apple' !

~nasreen

Troubled Waters

On the Shore a washed away Boat
Giant Waves coming crashing in'
A scary sight to my Eyes

~ nasreen

The unspoken

Hand in Hand they Walked
Fingers entwined to silent communication
Revealing the unspoken
How scandalous can Love be...!?
For she was just a dream

~ nasreen

My Daughter

The Rose that blossomed in my Garden
The sweet Melody of my Heart

My sincere Love
As beautiful as the Summer Blossoms

A perfect Red Rose in all it's sense
Everlasting happiness to my Soul

My strength when am sad and lonely
'In illness you are besides me'

My daily Smile
My courage

My Rainbow
My Fragrance

Only yesterday I held you in my Arms
Today you sit in my Lap

Your glistening Eyes speak the language of my Heart
For Mama always knows

My Precious
I will always love you .

(A birthday Poem for my daughter - 13th Feb. 1993)

~ nasreen

The Last Leaves

A sudden change in Weather
Winter chill spreading far and beyond
The last Leaves falling off one by one
Leaving the Trees almost barren
Looking like Skeletons under the dark Skies
Bringing a strange calmness
Autumn colours are no longer

~ nasreen

Sounds of my Garden

Cheerful day as the Sun rises
Beautiful Blossoms in my Garden
Bumble Bees collecting Nectar

~ nasreen

Unsolved Mystery

Beyond my thoughts a hidden memoir
My friend Jessica the vanishing Damsel

Leaving behind her Tears and laughter in a Diary
As I read page by page am dumbfounded

Unleashing her painful past
The Ink must have flowed fast on Paper

Scribbling unspoken Words
A love that was never to be

Sailing off to another Land
He was in search of Adventure

Never to be seen again
Every Dawn and Dusk she was left counting the Days

~nasreen

Sudden Reaction

Seductively rubbing her Feet
A surprise look she gave
Taken aback at his behaviour
She jumped to her Feet
Walking off instantly

~nasreen

Earth my Mother

Grow a Tree in my Womb
My Lungs for the Oxygen
For Life is precious on this Planet
Let not the Oceans rise
Swallowing everything in its site
Climate change would be a terrible devastation
For the end of the World will be nigh
'No one' I say No one will save us than'

~nasreen

Reality check

Absence of a loved one
Is the reality of the Souls
More broken with Pain

~nasreen

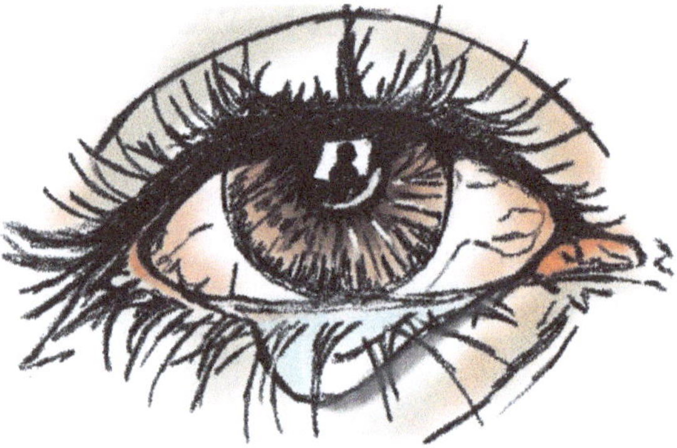

Tears Tears

Overwhelmed by hurt and Pain
Tears running down her Cheeks
A lonely Orphaned Child

~nasreen

The Single Rose

Sweet Love
Gentle Love
Silent Whispers echoing in my Soul
In harmony with my true feelings
For he had left me lonely
Now I would re-consider
Love isn't Real if love can't wait
You and I are just another heartbreak Story
For I thought you loved me

~nasreen

Bundle of Joy

Tiny Feet popping from a Blanket
Mama's Bundle of Joy
Filling every void in her Life

~ nasreen

Shadows Shadows

Walking on the Streets of Paris
Shadows following at Twilight
Each one with it's own Life Story

~nasreen

Broken Pieces

Broken Pieces of my Heart, sewn together

~nasreen

Beautiful Blossoms

A Vase full of vibrant colours
Sitting on a Shelf
Adding a cheerful message

~nasreen

Pain

Drowning in a Glass of Liquor
As if her Pain would seize from a broken Heartache

Glass after Glass she downed
Wasting her Life away

Feeling sick and nauseous
Her vision blinded temporarily

Again, and again she calling her Lover
'You hopeless fool' You left me for another'!

Tears running down her cheeks
First Ray of Sunshine and she knocks out on the
Settee

~nasreen

Lè Paris

Bonsoir Bonsoir...Beautiful Paris
She kept whispering to herself

Alone on the Streets recollecting her old self
Not a Soul around ...

Darkness befell and a cold chill brushing her
'I must keep going...' I must keep ...!?

Suddenly a Taxi stops by
Stepping in and never to be heard of again

~nasreen

Suicide

Torn from grief of a Lover
She ran to the edge of the Cliff
Suicide on her Mind

~nasreen

Time

As my Life ticks away
The Hour Glass bringing a new Dawn

My perilous journey into the future
As Darkness brings Sunshine

A beautiful Modern BIG BEN
I hear it's loud Chimes

Suddenly striking 12 Midnight
Ding Dooooong.!

Shaking my wits
My Ears aching to the loud Bells

Running to shut my apartment Window
Ohhh a beautiful scenario to the the Modern Clock

~nasreen

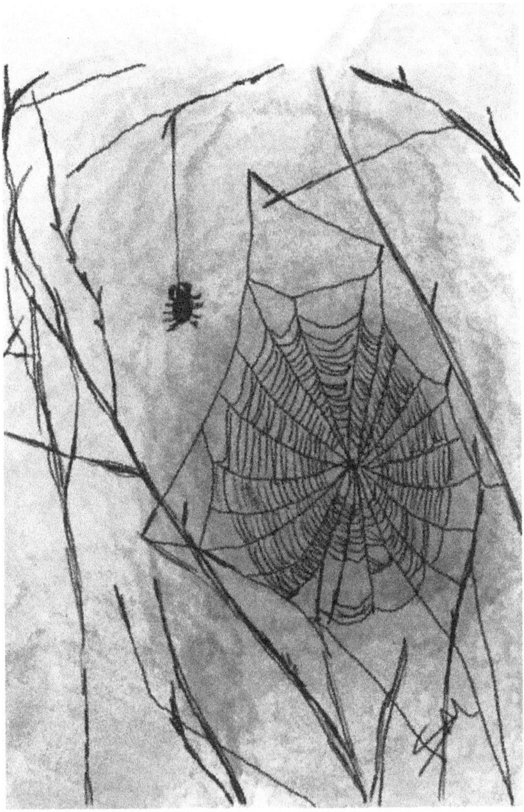

The Spider's Web

As I stroll in the Morning Hours
Hidden amongst the Bushes

I chance upon a Web
My Mind a bit confused

Studying the Web
Perfect weave

Thoughts crossing my Mind
I weaved my Life's Web too

Pain and Tears is what I weaved
My broken self now a nobody

Life isn't fair
My wrongs and rights

A judgement to my short Life
A painful ending but who are you to judge

~ nasreen

Ek Phool

Masum si Kali mere Daman mein
Khusboo Jese ek Gulab ki Kali
Khubsoorat hei uss ka andaz
Churah liya mera dil aur uss ke baba ka

Hatho mein utah kar Baba ne kaha
'Ajj mein mukamal hu'
Tofa diya sath jahno ke Malik ne
Naam se pukara " Saher Noor"

Apne chote hatho se Mama ko chuha
Hans pardhi mein, khushi ke Ansoo bahaye
Meri Godh bari uss pak zath ne itne salo ke badh
Duae mang kar paya app ko hum ne

Hamare Sar ka Taj, hamari har khushi
Hamari har sans
Hamari har tamanaye
Hamari dil ki dharkan

Ankho ki Roshni
Khwabo ki muskarat
Khilte raho sadah dua hei hamari
App he hei hamari zindagi ka ek maqsad jine ka

Acknowledgement

My sincerest thanks to Saher Malik, My daughter for putting a lot of effort in drawing the illustrations and helping me to compile "Where Whispers Echo", and also creating the cover design.

And also My sincerest thanks goes to BlueRose Publishers, New Delhi India, for spending a lot of their valuable time on compiling "Where Whispers Echo", and special thanks to the Editor.

~nasreen